CD INCLUDED

HAL•LEONARD
BIG BAND
PLAY-ALONG
VOLUME 6

# LATIN

GUITAR

T0082981

ISBN 978-1-4234-5878-4

HAL•LEONARD®
CORPORATION
7777 W. BLUEMOUND RD. P.O. BOX 13819 MILWAUKEE, WI 53213

Visit Hal Leonard Online at
www.halleonard.com

# ÁGUA DE BEBER
## (WATER TO DRINK)

Guitar

English Words by NORMAN GIMBEL
Portuguese Words by VINICIUS De MORAES
Music by ANTONIO CARLOS JOBIM
Arranged by JOHN BERRY

# AT THE MAMBO INN

By GRACE SAMPSON, BOBBY WOODLEN
and MARIO BAUZA
Arranged by MICHAEL PHILIP MOSSMAN

Guitar

THIS PAGE HAS BEEN LEFT BLANK TO ACCOMMODATE PAGE TURNS.

# BÉSAME MUCHO
## (KISS ME MUCH)

Guitar

Music and Spanish Words by CONSUELO VELAZQUEZ
English Words by SUNNY SKYLAR
Arranged by RICK STITZEL

# THE LOOK OF LOVE

Words by HAL DAVID
Music by BURT BACHARACH
Arranged by JOHN BERRY

Guitar

# MAMBO No. 5
## (A LITTLE BIT OF...)

Guitar

Original Music by DAMASO PEREZ PRADO
Words by LOU BEGA and ZIPPY
Arranged by ROGER HOLMES

# MAS QUE NADA

Words and Music by
**JORGE BEN**
Arranged by MARK TAYLOR

Guitar

# ONE NOTE SAMBA
## (SAMBA DE UMA NOTA SO)

Guitar

Original Lyrics by NEWTON MENDONCA
English Lyrics by ANTONIO CARLOS JOBIM
Music by ANTONIO CARLOS JOBIM
Arranged by PAUL MURTHA

# QUIET NIGHTS OF QUIET STARS
## (CORCOVADO)

Guitar

English Words by GENE LEES
Original Words and Music by ANTONIO CARLOS JOBIM
Arranged by PAUL MURTHA

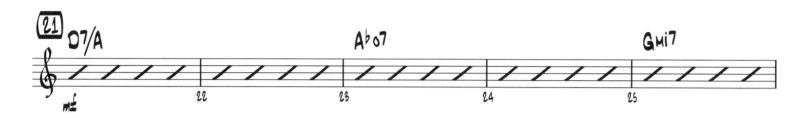

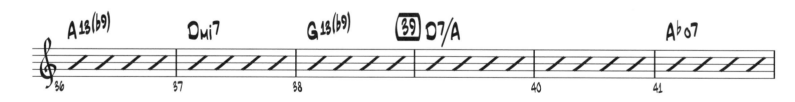

# RAN KAN KAN

GUITAR

By TITO PUENTE
Arranged by RICK STITZEL

21

# ST. THOMAS

Guitar

By SONNY ROLLINS
Arranged by MARK TAYLOR

# THE BIG BAND PLAY-ALONG SERIES

These revolutionary play-along packs are great products for those who want a big band sound to back up their instrument, without the pressure of playing solo. They're perfect for current players and for those former players who want to get back in the swing!

## Each volume includes:

- Easy-to-read, authentic big band arrangements

- Professional recordings on CD of all the big band instruments, including the lead part

- Editions for alto sax, tenor sax, trumpet, trombone, guitar, piano, bass, and drums

## 1. SWING FAVORITES

April in Paris • I've Got You Under My Skin • In the Mood • It Don't Mean a Thing (If It Ain't Got That Swing) • Route 66 • Speak Low • Stompin' at the Savoy • Tangerine • This Can't Be Love • Until I Met You (Corner Pocket).

| | | |
|---|---|---|
| 07011313 | Alto Sax | $14.95 |
| 07011314 | Tenor Sax | $14.95 |
| 07011315 | Trumpet | $14.95 |
| 07011316 | Trombone | $14.95 |
| 07011317 | Guitar | $14.95 |
| 07011318 | Piano | $14.95 |
| 07011319 | Bass | $14.95 |
| 07011320 | Drums | $14.95 |

## 2. POPULAR HITS

Ain't No Mountain High Enough • Brick House • Copacabana (At the Copa) • Evil Ways • I Heard It Through the Grapevine • On Broadway • Respect • Street Life • Yesterday • Zoot Suit Riot.

| | | |
|---|---|---|
| 07011321 | Alto Sax | $14.95 |
| 07011322 | Tenor Sax | $14.95 |
| 07011323 | Trumpet | $14.95 |
| 07011324 | Trombone | $14.95 |
| 07011325 | Guitar | $14.95 |
| 07011326 | Piano | $14.95 |
| 07011327 | Bass | $14.95 |
| 07011328 | Drums | $14.95 |

## 3. DUKE ELLINGTON

Caravan • Chelsea Bridge • Cotton Tail • I'm Beginning to See the Light • I'm Just a Lucky So and So • In a Mellow Tone • In a Sentimental Mood • Mood Indigo • Satin Doll • Take the "A" Train.

| | | |
|---|---|---|
| 00843086 | Alto Sax | $14.95 |
| 00843087 | Tenor Sax | $14.95 |
| 00843088 | Trumpet | $14.95 |
| 00843089 | Trombone | $14.95 |
| 00843090 | Guitar | $14.95 |
| 00843091 | Piano | $14.95 |
| 00843092 | Bass | $14.95 |
| 00843093 | Drums | $14.95 |

## 4. JAZZ CLASSICS

Bags' Groove • Blue 'N Boogie • Blue Train (Blue Trane) • Doxy • Four • Moten Swing • Oleo • Song for My Father • Stolen Moments • Straight No Chaser.

| | | |
|---|---|---|
| 00843094 | Alto Sax | $14.95 |
| 00843095 | Tenor Sax | $14.95 |
| 00843096 | Trumpet | $14.95 |
| 00843097 | Trombone | $14.95 |
| 00843098 | Guitar | $14.95 |
| 00843099 | Piano | $14.95 |
| 00843100 | Bass | $14.95 |
| 00843101 | Drums | $14.95 |

## 5. CHRISTMAS FAVORITES

Baby, It's Cold Outside • The Christmas Song • Feliz Navidad • I'll Be Home for Christmas • Let It Snow! Let It Snow! Let It Snow! • Little Saint Nick • My Favorite Things • Silver Bells • This Christmas • White Christmas.

| | | |
|---|---|---|
| 00843118 | Alto Sax | $14.95 |
| 00843119 | Tenor Sax | $14.95 |
| 00843120 | Trumpet | $14.95 |
| 00843121 | Trombone | $14.95 |
| 00843122 | Guitar | $14.95 |
| 00843123 | Piano | $14.95 |
| 00843124 | Bass | $14.95 |
| 00843125 | Drums | $14.95 |

## 6. LATIN

Água De Beber (Water to Drink) • At the Mambo Inn • Bésame Mucho (Kiss Me Much) • The Look of Love • Mambo No. 5 (A Little Bit of...) • Mas Que Nada • One Note Samba (Samba De Uma Nota So) • Quiet Nights of Quiet Stars (Corcovado) • Ran Kan Kan • St. Thomas.

| | | |
|---|---|---|
| 00843126 | Alto Sax | $14.99 |
| 00843127 | Tenor Sax | $14.99 |
| 00843128 | Trumpet | $14.99 |
| 00843129 | Trombone | $14.99 |
| 00843130 | Guitar | $14.99 |
| 00843131 | Piano | $14.99 |
| 00843132 | Bass | $14.99 |
| 00843133 | Drums | $14.99 |

## 7. STANDARDS

Autumn Leaves • Easy to Love (You'd Be So Easy to Love) • Georgia on My Mind • Harlem Nocturne • It Might As Well Be Spring • Ja-Da • Just in Time • My Funny Valentine • Night Song • On the Sunny Side of the Street.

| | | |
|---|---|---|
| 00843134 | Alto Sax | $14.99 |
| 00843135 | Tenor Sax | $14.99 |
| 00843136 | Trumpet | $14.99 |
| 00843137 | Trombone | $14.99 |
| 00843138 | Guitar | $14.99 |
| 00843139 | Piano | $14.99 |
| 00843140 | Bass | $14.99 |
| 00843141 | Drums | $14.99 |

FOR MORE INFORMATION, SEE YOUR LOCAL MUSIC DEALER, OR WRITE TO:

HAL•LEONARD® CORPORATION
7777 W. BLUEMOUND RD. P.O. BOX 13819
MILWAUKEE, WISCONSIN 53213

www.halleonard.com

Prices, contents, and availability subject to change without notice.

0509